# GOLDEN STATE
# WARRIORS

by Rob Tricchinelli

THIS BOOK CONTAINS AT LEAST 10% RECYCLED MATERIALS.

Editor: Dave McMahon
Copy Editor: Anna Comstock
Series design and cover production: Christa Schneider
Interior production: Carol Castro

**Photo Credits:** Duane Burleson/AP Images, cover; Paul Vathis/AP Images, 1, 42 (middle); Rusty Kennedy/AP Images, 4, 42 (bottom); Roger Photo Archive/Getty Images, 7, 27, 43 (top); AP Images, 9, 12, 16, 19, 20, 23; NBA Photos/NBAE/Getty Images, 10, 29, 42 (top); WGI/AP Images, 14; Focus on Sport/Getty Images, 24; Gloria Ferniz/AP Images, 30, 43 (middle); Ray Stubblebine/AP Images, 33; George Nikitin/AP Images, 34; Chris Gardner/AP Images, 36; Marcio Jose Sanchez/AP Images, 39, 43 (bottom); Peter Morgan/AP Images, 40; Dino Vournas/AP Images, 44; Rocky Widner/NBAE/Getty Images, 47

**Library of Congress Cataloging-in-Publication Data**
Tricchinelli, Rob, 1985-
 Golden State Warriors / by Rob Tricchinelli.
   p. cm. -- (Inside the NBA)
 Includes index.
 ISBN 978-1-61783-157-7
 1. Golden State Warriors (Basketball team)--History--Juvenile literature. I. Title.
 GV885.52.G64T75 2012
 796.323'640979461--dc23
                    2011020288

# TABLE OF CONTENTS

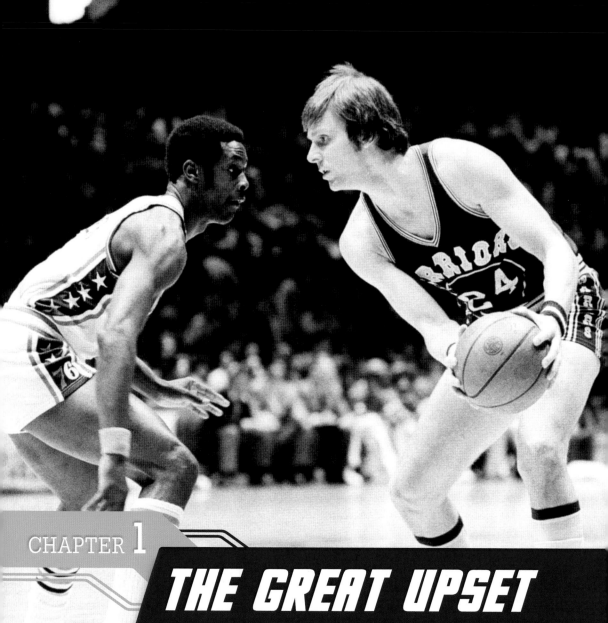

CHAPTER 1

# THE GREAT UPSET

# T

he Golden State Warriors thrilled their fans during the 1974–75 National Basketball Association (NBA) season. The Warriors had won 44 games in the previous season, but that was not enough to advance to the playoffs.

Their playoff status changed with the 1974–75 campaign, though. The Warriors finished with the best regular-season record in the Western Conference, 48–34. They won the Pacific Division. Now they had their sights set on winning their first NBA championship.

Coach Al Attles had formed a deep team to support high-scoring forward Rick Barry. Attles traded center/forward Nate Thurmond, who was in his early thirties. In return, the Warriors got 26-year-old Clifford Ray. Ray was known as a great rebounder. Forward

The Warriors' Rick Barry, *right*, was named MVP of the 1975 NBA Finals. Barry, shown keeping the ball away from the Philadelphia 76ers' Fred Carter in February 1976, was a 12-time All-Star.

# AL ATTLES

Al Attles is a proud lifetime Warrior. He played for the Warriors from 1960 to 1971. His playing career spanned the team's move from Philadelphia. He also became the Warriors' coach in January 1970, when he started as a player/coach.

Attles was the second African American coach to win an NBA title, after Bill Russell. He was also the general manager of the Warriors for three years. He later became an active face of the team in the local community. Attles's career included the 1975 championship and two other NBA Finals appearances. He won 557 games as a coach and had a winning record in both the regular season and postseason.

Although he is not involved with running the team anymore, Attles still attends every Warriors home game. With more than 50 consecutive years as a Warriors employee, he has the longest unbroken streak of service to any NBA team.

Jamaal Wilkes, along with guards Butch Beard and Charles Johnson, averaged at least 10 points per game that season.

The Warriors faced the Seattle SuperSonics in the opening round of the play-offs. The Sonics were coached by NBA legend Bill Russell. They also had two effective scorers in Spencer Haywood and Fred Brown. The Sonics were a young, quick team, but the Warriors beat them in six games.

Golden State next took on the Chicago Bulls, who had Thurmond. The Warriors fell behind three games to two. They had to beat Chicago on the road in Game 6 just to stay alive. They hustled on defense and prevailed 86–72. In Game 7, the Warriors defended their home court, 83–79, and advanced to the NBA Finals.

Coach Al Attles guided the Warriors to the NBA title in 1975. Attles played for the Warriors from 1960 to 1971 and still attends every home game.

The Washington Bullets awaited in the Finals. They had All-Stars Elvin Hayes and Wes Unseld. Unseld led the league in rebounds per game that season. Washington had rattled off 60 wins in the regular season and had been effective in the playoffs.

## Jamaal Wilkes

Jamaal Wilkes was only a rookie when the Warriors won it all in 1975, but he played like a veteran. His 14.2 points and 8.2 rebounds per game both were second on the team. Wilkes left the team in 1977 and went on to a productive career with the Los Angeles Lakers and the Los Angeles Clippers.

The Warriors picked up a surprising 101–95 win on the road in Game 1. The next two games were at Golden State. In Game 2, the Warriors had a 92–91 lead with six seconds left. Washington missed two shots that would have won the game, so the Warriors once again prevailed. Barry scored 38 points in Game 3. The Warriors won another close one, 109–101.

Leading the series three games to none, Golden State had some room for error. In Game 4, the team played carelessly to start the game. The Warriors fell behind by more than a dozen points. Attles was ejected from the game in the first quarter, but the team played tight defense with Attles gone. Beard iced a 96–95 Golden State victory with a pair of late free throws. The Warriors were NBA champions. They had swept the heavily favored Bullets and risen to basketball's highest level.

"It has to be the greatest upset in the history of the NBA Finals," said Barry, who was the Finals' Most Valuable Player (MVP). "It was like a fairy-tale season. Everything just fell into place. It's something I'll treasure for the rest of my life."

The Warriors followed up their championship with two consecutive playoff appearances, but they did not return to the NBA Finals. Each time, the series that eliminated

## Phil Smith

*Phil Smith was a rookie during the championship season. He had six solid seasons with Golden State. A guard who played college at the University of San Francisco, Smith was a two-time NBA All-Star. He also made the All-NBA second team and the All-Defensive second team in 1976. He was originally from San Francisco and was a fan favorite.*

Phil Smith greets fans at the San Francisco airport after the Warriors returned from winning the NBA title against the Washington Bullets. Smith was known for his defensive play.

Golden State went to a full seven games. And their 1976 playoff defeat to the Phoenix Suns included a loss in two overtimes. The Warriors could not finish, and their championship successes would soon be nothing but a memory.

# CHAPTER 2

# PHILADELPHIA'S FINEST

T he roots of the Golden State Warriors begin thousands of miles away from California, which is nicknamed "the Golden State." The team's story begins in Philadelphia, Pennsylvania, in 1946. And it does not begin in the NBA.

When the Philadelphia Warriors first took to the court, they were part of the Basketball Association of America (BAA). The BAA started with the 1946–47 season.

Warriors forward Joe Fulks stole the show that first season. He led the league in

Paul Arizin, *left*, and Joe Fulks played key roles for the Philadelphia Warriors. The Warriors later moved to California.

Eddie Gottlieb, *left*, owner of the Philadelphia Warriors, was honored for his outstanding contributions to basketball in 1957. Frank McGuire, *right*, later coached the Warriors.

scoring with 23.2 points per game. No one else scored more than 17 points per game.

Philadelphia had the fourth-best record of any of the 11 BAA teams that first year. They defeated the St. Louis Bombers and the New York Knickerbockers in the play-offs. That sent the Warriors to the BAA Finals against the Chicago Stags.

The Warriors won the first game at home. Fulks made eight shots in a row in the fourth quarter. He finished with 37 points. The press called Fulks's game "the greatest shooting exhibition ever seen on the arena floor."

After another win at home, Philadelphia won a third game on the road. Philadelphia led the series three games to none

**Eddie Gottlieb**

Eddie Gottlieb was the coach of the Warriors in the team's early days. He eventually became the team's owner. He also took a leadership role in the NBA and helped to create and change rules in order to keep the game exciting. Today, the NBA's Rookie of the Year award is called the Eddie Gottlieb Trophy.

against the Stags. Chicago won 74–73 in Game 4, and the series went back to Philadelphia.

Game 5 was very close. The score was 80–80 late in the game. Fulks racked up 34 points, but teammate Howie Dallmar delivered the glory. Dallmar made a 30-foot shot with less than a minute to go.

The Warriors won 83–80 and captured the first BAA title. With Eddie Gottlieb staying on as coach, the team's success continued during the 1947–48 season.

Philadelphia went 27–21 and beat the St. Louis Bombers to make another trip to the BAA Finals.

After winning Game 1 over the Baltimore Bullets, the Warriors blew a big lead and lost Game 2. The Bullets won three of the next four games and prevented the Warriors from repeating as champions.

The Warriors then lost in the first round of the BAA playoffs to end the 1948–49 season. After that season, the BAA and its 12 teams joined with the National Basketball League to create the NBA. The NBA began play in 1949 with 17 teams.

Philadelphia lost in the first round of the playoffs in each of the NBA's first three seasons. The team then missed the playoffs the next three years. In the 1952 playoffs, four future Hall of Famers were on the team. Fulks, Paul Arizin, Neil Johnston, and Andy Phillip all had standout careers.

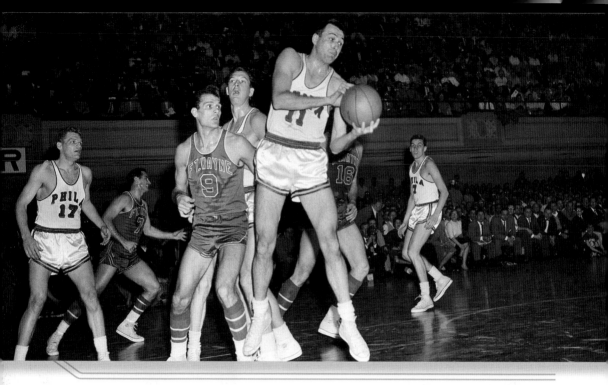

Paul Arizin (11) of the Philadelphia Warriors grabs a rebound against the Fort Wayne Pistons during the 1956 NBA Finals in Philadelphia.

### Tom Gola

*Standing 6 feet 6 inches tall, Tom Gola was a forward and center in college at La Salle University in Philadelphia. But when he turned pro, he became a forward. At that position he played farther away from the basket. He was a great two-way player. He used his size to attack the basket and rebound. Gola also could handle the ball in the same way that much smaller players could. He did it all for the Warriors in the late 1950s and early 1960s. He was inducted into the Basketball Hall of Fame in 1976.*

For the 1955–56 season, Arizin was back after spending two years in the military. He scored 24.2 points per game. Teammate Tom Gola was a rookie sensation. And Johnston averaged more than 20 points per game for the fourth year in a row.

Their 45–27 record was the best in the NBA. They beat the Syracuse Nationals in the playoffs to make their first appearance in the NBA Finals. There, they faced the Fort Wayne Pistons.

The teams traded wins in the first two games, but Philadelphia dominated after that. In front of a home crowd in Game 3, Arizin scored 27 points, and Johnston added 20 more as the Warriors won, 100–96. Arizin poured in another 30 points in Game 4. He drained 26 in Game 5. The Warriors won both games and claimed their first NBA championship.

The Warriors made the playoffs the following two years, but then missed the playoffs entirely in 1959. Later that year, the Warriors drafted a dynamic 7-foot center named Wilt Chamberlain. Philadelphia made the playoffs three years in a row beginning with the 1959–60 season, but big changes were coming.

## WILT'S CENTURY CLUB

In March 1962, Wilt Chamberlain poured in 100 points in the Warriors' 169–147 victory over the New York Knicks.

The young center regularly dominated play under the basket. But that night, he was nearly unstoppable. He made 36 of his 63 shots from the field. He also sank 28 of 32 free throws, even though on average he only made about half of his free throws during his entire career. Chamberlain's night broke his own record of 78 points in a game. No other player has scored 100 in a game through the 2010–11 season.

Of all the records and accomplishments over his career, Chamberlain might be best known for his triple-digit scoring that night. After the game, he held up a piece of paper with "100" written on it and posed for what is now one of the most famous NBA photos ever taken.

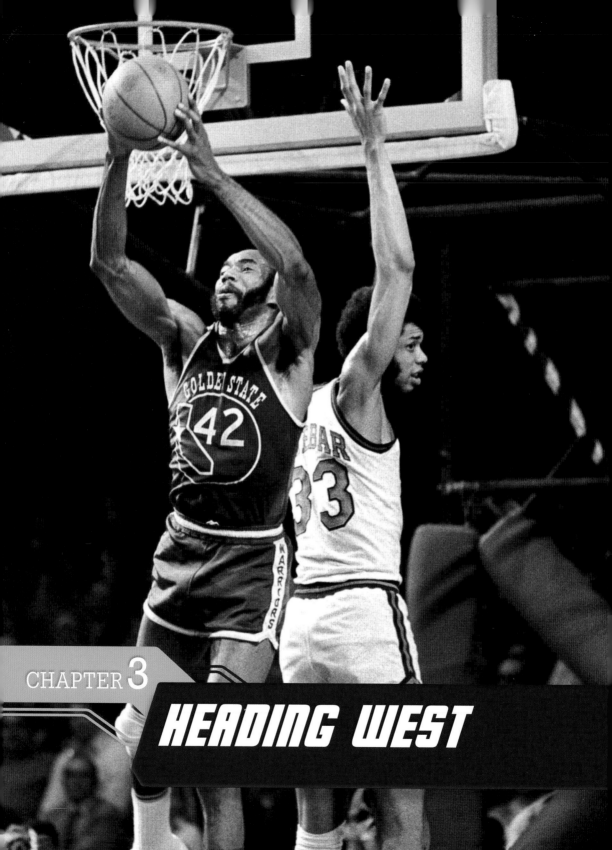

# CHAPTER 3

# HEADING WEST

**I**n 1962, a group of businessmen led by Franklin Mieuli purchased the Warriors. The new owners moved the team from Philadelphia to San Francisco, California. No longer located in the eastern United States, the San Francisco Warriors moved into the NBA's Western Division.

In their first season in San Francisco, the Warriors stumbled to a 31–49 record in 1962–63. They missed the playoffs entirely.

The next year, a new coach and a new player provided a needed lift. Coach Alex Hannum turned his team into a bruising squad. Center Wilt Chamberlain, standing 7 feet tall, and Nate Thurmond, a 6-foot-11-inch rookie presented problems for opponents. In 1963–64, the Warriors exploded to a 48–32 record to win the Western Division. They had the best scoring defense in the league. That

The Warriors' Nate Thurmond (42) keeps his position to collect a rebound against the Bucks' Kareem Abdul-Jabbar during the 1972 playoffs.

means they allowed the fewest points per game.

The Warriors survived an exciting seven-game series in the Western Division finals against the St. Louis Hawks. Next, they met the Boston Celtics in the NBA Finals. The Warriors did not have much success against the Celtics. Chamberlain, Thurmond, and forward Tom Meschery had impressive playoff statistics. Those individual performances, however, did not matter. Boston won the series in five games.

The Warriors did not have much success following the 1963–64 season. In 1964–65 they only won 17 games. They were struggling on the business end, too. During the season, San Francisco traded Chamberlain back to Philadelphia. That city was now the home of a different NBA team, the 76ers. The next year was not much better for the Warriors. Hannum did not return as coach after that.

Bill Sharman replaced Hannum as coach for the 1966–67 season. Chamberlain was gone, but Rick Barry was ready to be a star. Barry was a skilled forward who could score. He also shot his free throws underhanded. It was

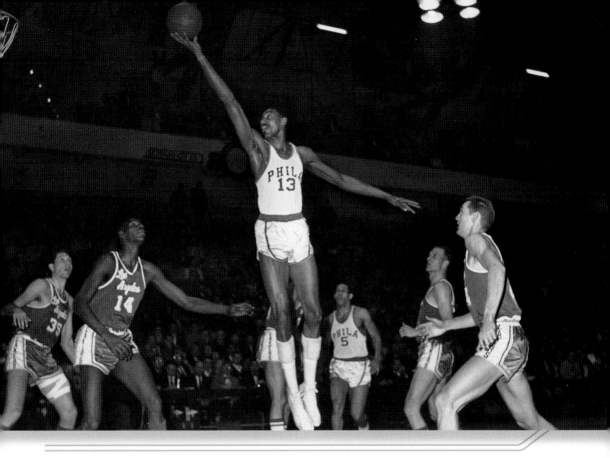

The Warriors' Wilt Chamberlain stretches for a basket against Los Angeles in 1961 at the Philadelphia Arena.

a unique technique for which he soon became known. Barry led the league in scoring in his second year with more than 35 points per game. The Warriors won the Western Division and topped the St. Louis Hawks to reach the NBA Finals.

In the Finals, the Warriors faced the Philadelphia 76ers.

The series was a battle of the old Philadelphia team versus the new one. Plus, Chamberlain played for the 76ers, and Hannum was their coach. Philadelphia had gone 68–13 in the regular season. That was the best record in the league. And they had knocked off the Celtics in the Eastern Division

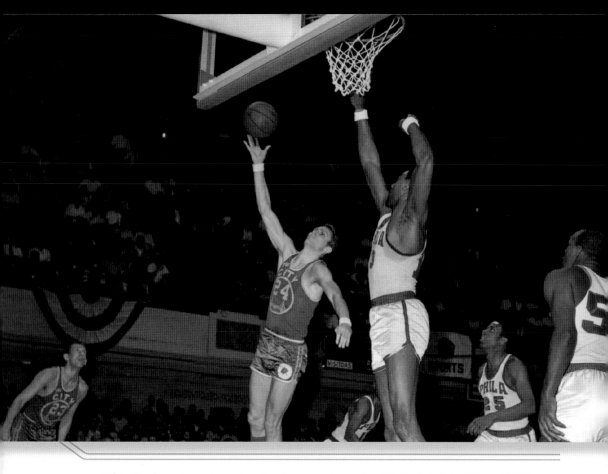

Rick Barry attempts a hook shot against the Philadelphia 76ers' Wilt Chamberlain in the 1967 playoffs.

## Barry Sits Out

*"Listen, if all 10 guys go up for a rebound, Rick will not only get it, but the other nine will somehow fall down and he will end up with a layup. The first exhibition game, he was so tired he looked as if he'd have to come out for oxygen every seven minutes, and he still got 52 points."*
—Larry Brown, Barry's teammate on the ABA's Oakland Oaks

finals. The 76ers won the first two games of the Finals at home and never looked back. San Francisco lost in six games. The Warriors had now come up short in the NBA Finals for the second time in four years.

Much of the excitement for Warriors fans wore off when Barry announced he would miss the 1967–68 season. Barry had a contract disagreement with the Warriors and sat out the last year of his NBA contract, so he went to play in the American Basketball Association (ABA) with the Oakland Oaks. The ABA was a rival league to the NBA that had started in 1967. Hannum was his coach with the Oaks.

Without Barry, the Warriors made the playoffs three times in four years but did not return to the NBA Finals. They advanced to the Western Division finals in 1968, but the Los Angeles Lakers swept them in that series.

George Lee replaced Sharman as coach for the 1968–69 season. Then the following season, Al Attles replaced Lee with 30 games left to play in the regular season.

The Warriors moved again in 1971. This time

## RICK BARRY

Rick Barry was one of the greatest forwards to ever play basketball. He was known for his shooting ability.

He also used his skills to get the ball to the basket in a variety of ways. Plus, he was a scoring machine. He was the only person to ever lead the country in scoring as a college player, in the NBA, and in the ABA.

He led the NBA in scoring average with 35.6 points per game in the 1966–67 season. He led the NBA in free throw shooting percentage six times.

He also did not tolerate mistakes from his teammates. Because of his attitude, he made few friends during his career.

Unlike their treatment of other superstars of his time, fans did not provide Barry with much support. Even so, his success on the court put him on 12 All-Star teams.

He was inducted into the Basketball Hall of Fame in 1987.

they moved across the San Francisco Bay to Oakland. They had been playing some of their games in previous seasons at the Oakland-Alameda County Coliseum Arena.

During the 1971–72 season, the team also played a few home games in San Diego. San Diego is located nearly 500 miles (800 km) away from Oakland. But they played no more in nearby San Francisco. They dropped the city from their name and became known as the Golden State Warriors. They were named after the state nickname of California.

The Golden State Warriors again qualified for the playoffs in their first two seasons in Oakland. In 1971–72, they lost in the first round of the playoffs to the Milwaukee Bucks for the second year in a row. The Bucks were led by rising star Kareem Abdul-Jabbar.

## Jerry Lucas

A 6-foot-8-inch forward out of Ohio State, Jerry Lucas played only parts of two seasons with San Francisco. But he made his mark during the 1969–70 and 1970–71 seasons. He was an accurate shooter and strong rebounder. He made the NBA All-Star Game in 1971 while with the Warriors. He also made the Basketball Hall of Fame in 1980.

Cazzie Russell, a forward/guard who had been the first pick in the 1966 NBA Draft, averaged 21.4 points per game in the first of his three seasons with the Warriors.

In the 1972–73 season playoffs, however, the Warriors got revenge on the Bucks in the Western Conference semifinals. Golden State defeated the Bucks in six games thanks to some solid play by Barry.

After playing in the ABA with three teams in four years, Barry had come back to the NBA for the 1972–73 season.

The Warriors' Cazzie Russell (32) and the Boston Celtics' Don Nelson go for a rebound in 1971. Nelson coached the Warriors for parts of 11 seasons.

Mieuli, the Warriors' owner, had persuaded him to return. "He vowed to do everything in his power to get me back," Barry said about Mieuli. "Thank goodness he did."

To get back to the NBA Finals, the Warriors had to face the Los Angeles Lakers. The Lakers edged Golden State in the first two games. Both games were in Los Angeles. The series then returned to Golden State's home court, but the Lakers crushed the Warriors 126–70 in Game 3.

Golden State won Game 4 at home, and the series returned to Los Angeles. The Lakers breezed by 10 points to advance to their 10th NBA Finals in 15 years. Los Angeles eventually lost in the Finals to the New York Knickerbockers.

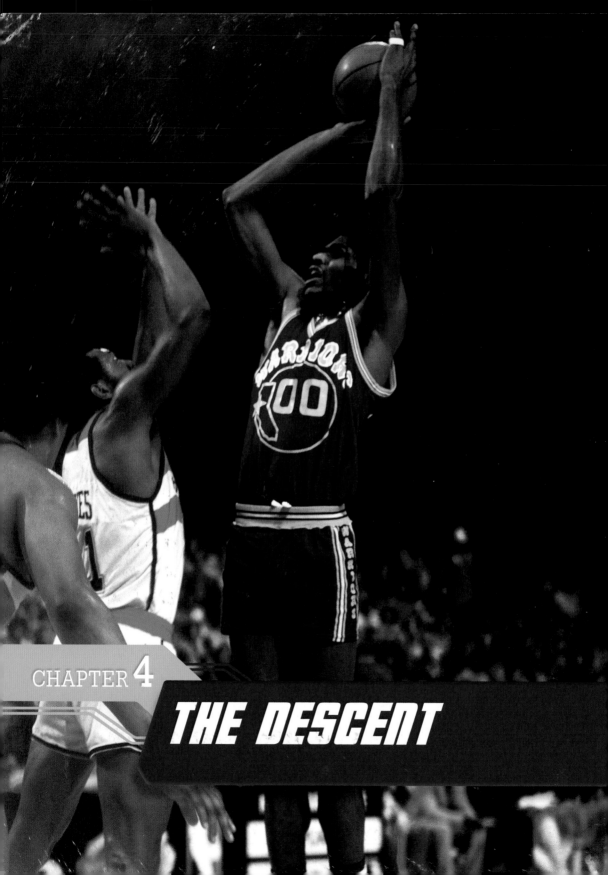

CHAPTER 4

# THE DESCENT

The Warriors had won the 1975 NBA championship with a young team that supported superstar Rick Barry. The young players included Jamaal Wilkes, George Johnson, and Butch Beard.

By 1977, those young players were gone. And a year later, Barry had departed. He finished his Hall of Fame career with the Houston Rockets.

When Barry left, the Warriors lost a big part of their identity. And although coach Al Attles had put together a team that won a championship, he was never again able to achieve the same kind of success. Golden State missed the playoffs by one game in the 1977–78 season, and then tumbled below .500 the next season. In the 1979–80 season, they were a miserable 24–58. That was the second-worst record in the NBA.

Robert Parish shoots against the Washington Bullets. Parish, nicknamed "The Chief," spent the first four seasons of his career with the Warriors.

## THE CHIEF

A native of Shreveport, Louisiana, Robert Parish started his career with Golden State, but got traded to Boston in 1980. With the Celtics, Parish won three NBA titles and went to the Finals twice more. He made the All-Star team nine times in an 11-year stretch.

At 7 feet 1 inches tall, Parish frequently was among the league's top 10 rebounders, and he had an effective short-range jump shot. He was a tough defender but was very soft-spoken off the court. Parish had the nickname "The Chief," after a tall, quiet character in a movie.

He was also very durable. He played in 1,611 career games, which is the most ever by a professional basketball player. Parish finished his playing days with the Charlotte Hornets and the Chicago Bulls. He won a fourth championship with the Bulls in 1997, his final year in the NBA. He was inducted into the Basketball Hall of Fame in 2003.

Bad luck struck again in the 1981–82 season, when the Warriors missed the playoffs by one game. A year later, they tumbled to 30–52. That dismal season would be Attles' last as Warriors coach. Johnny Bach replaced him.

Bach's three years as coach were forgettable. The team only won 89 games combined in those years, and twice finished last in the Western Conference. Attles had moved from coach to general manager, but struggled to rebuild the team in that role.

The Warriors had young, talented players during this poor stretch. But they seemed unable to keep many of them for more than a few years.

Bad trades also doomed the team. Robert Parish was a tough young center, but he was traded to Boston and went on to a Hall of Fame career.

Joe Barry Carroll, *left*, and World B. Free, *center*, were solid players for the Warriors under coach Al Attles, *right*, in the early 1980s.

Bernard King was an All-Star for the Warriors in the 1981–82 season, but he was traded away for Micheal Ray Richardson before the 1982–83 season started. Richardson played for the Warriors for about half of one season before being traded again.

### Joe Barry Carroll

*When the Warriors traded away Robert Parish, they got a first-round draft pick in return. It turned out to be the first overall pick, and with it, they picked Joe Barry Carroll. He was a big man and a good shot blocker who had a few solid years with Golden State. The Warriors traded him in 1987, and the rest of his career was shortened by injuries.*

**J**oe Barry Carroll, Sleepy Floyd, and Chris Mullin led the Warriors back to the play-offs in the 1986–87 season. It was coach George Karl's first year on their bench. Golden State finished fifth in the Western Conference with a 42–40 record. They opened the playoffs against the Utah Jazz. The Jazz was only two games better than the Warriors during the regular season.

Things looked bleak when the Jazz won the first two games at home. Utah traveled to Golden State needing only one game to advance. But the Warriors had other ideas. They blew out the Jazz in Game 3 and nipped them by four points in Game 4. The series went back to Utah for a deciding Game 5. The Warriors won 118–113 to set up a showdown with the Los Angeles Lakers in the Western Conference semifinals.

The Lakers were the best team in the NBA during the

The Warriors' Chris Mullin (17) goes up for a shot past the San Antonio Spurs' Greg Anderson. Mullin was named to the Basketball Hall of Fame in 2011.

## CHRIS MULLIN

After struggling to adjust to life on the West Coast, native New Yorker Chris Mullin thrived in coach Don Nelson's fast-paced system. He made five consecutive All-Star Games from 1989 through 1993.

Mullin was among the league's leaders in scoring, three-point shooting, and steals when the Warriors were regularly making the playoffs.

He was also a member of the USA's Olympic Basketball team known as the "Dream Team," which won the gold medal at the 1992 Summer Olympics. Injuries slowed Mullin later in his career and the Warriors traded him in 1997 to the Indiana Pacers.

He returned to Golden State in 2000 and retired shortly after as a Warrior. Mullin also spent seven years as part of Golden State's management before leaving in 2009. He was elected to the Basketball Hall of Fame in 2011.

regular season with a 65–17 record. They were loaded with talent. They had MVP Magic Johnson, James Worthy, and Kareem Abdul-Jabbar. Los Angeles won big in the first three games of the series. They were looking for a sweep on Golden State's home court.

But Floyd would not be denied in Game 4. He seemed ready to take on the Lakers by himself. His performance matched his desire. Floyd scored 29 points in the fourth quarter as the Warriors won 129–121. He made 12 shots from the field in the fourth quarter and scored 39 points in the second half. His points in a quarter, field goals in a quarter, and points in a half are NBA records. Sportswriters called Floyd's performance "electric."

Unfortunately, Golden State was overmatched by the

Eric "Sleepy" Floyd (21) drives toward the basket around the New York Knicks' Chris McNealy in 1987.

Lakers in Game 5. Los Angeles won that game 118–106. The Lakers then swept the Seattle SuperSonics in the Western Conference finals and beat the Boston Celtics in the NBA Finals.

Still, the Warriors seemed to take a promising step forward by making the playoffs for the first time in 10 years. They

## So Sleepy

Eric Floyd got the name "Sleepy" because of his droopy eyelids. He was anything but sleepy on the court, though. He was a quick guard who could score in bunches. He averaged more than 17 points per game in parts of six seasons with Golden State. Floyd made the All-Star Game in 1987. That was his last full season as a Warrior. He was traded to Houston during the 1987–88 season, along with Joe Barry Carroll.

Tim Hardaway, *right*, goes up for the basket as the New Jersey Nets' Yinka Dare defends. Hardaway gave the Warriors a strong presence at point guard for 5 1/2 seasons.

## Don Nelson

Don Nelson, nicknamed "Nellie," played 14 NBA seasons, mostly with the Boston Celtics. He also spent 31 seasons as a coach. Nelson coached the Warriors for seven years starting in the late 1980s, and again for four years in the late 2000s. He retired as a coach with 1,335 wins. That was the most all-time. He was the NBA's Coach of the Year three times. And although he won five NBA championships as a player, he never captured a title as a coach.

looked to build on it in 1987–88. Instead, they took an even bigger step backward. They went 20–62 that season. That was their worst record since the 1960s.

Players had personal issues that affected their play on the court. Team management basically gave up on the season and tried to rebuild for the future. They traded away Purvis Short,

Carroll, and Floyd to the Rockets in two separate deals before the season was half over.

The Warriors drafted Mitch Richmond in 1988 and Tim Hardaway in 1989. Both were future All-Stars. Karl was gone as coach after the team had posted a 16–48 record.

New coach Don Nelson installed a fast-paced offense in 1988–89 and his teams scored at a high rate. With the young talent and Mullin's steady shot, the Warriors were poised to improve.

From 1988 to 1994, the Warriors were among the league's leaders in points scored per game. It was no coincidence that Golden State made the playoffs four times in that span, too. The Warriors, however, never made it past the Western Conference semifinals.

Nelson traded Richmond in 1991, but he was trying to

## Mitch Richmond

Guard Mitch Richmond showed early promise for the Warriors. He was the NBA Rookie of the Year in 1989, but got traded to the Sacramento Kings before he realized his full potential. With the Kings, Richmond's career took off. He made six straight All-Star games and averaged more than 20 points per game in seven seasons with Sacramento. He finished his career with the Washington Wizards and the Los Angeles Lakers. When he retired, Richmond had more than 20,000 career points. That ranks among the top 40 all-time for a career through 2010–11.

build something better. Nelson had traded to get Chris Webber, and he drafted Latrell Sprewell. Both were flashy young players who fit his system. Even so, the Phoenix Suns swept the Warriors in the first round of the 1994 playoffs. Any hope for a championship would soon turn to disappointment.

JASON RICHARDSON

# CHAPTER 6

# FACING MORE TOUGH TIMES

**T**he Warriors' Chris Webber was named the NBA's Rookie of the Year for the 1993–94 season. He was big at 6 feet 10 inches tall, but he handled the ball and passed extremely well for his size.

Coach Don Nelson wanted to use Webber as a big man inside. But Webber himself wanted to play away from the basket more and use his other skills. Because of these differences, the player and coach did not get along. Their disagreements became so bad that the Warriors traded Webber to the Washington Bullets after just one season.

This was the first sign that trouble was coming for the Warriors. The Warriors started the 1994–95 season 14–31, and Nelson was fired. They stumbled the rest of the year and finished 26–56. That was not exactly the follow-up their fans had anticipated.

Their season took an even lower turn at a practice in December 1997. Warriors

Guard Jason Richardson flies through the air during the 2002 Slam Dunk Contest. Richardson made an impact on the Warriors from 2001 to 2007.

guard Latrell Sprewell got into a heated argument with coach P. J. Carlesimo. Sprewell attacked the coach by grabbing him around the neck and throwing him down on the ground. Sprewell choked the coach until his teammates pulled him off. He was suspended for the rest of the season by the NBA and never played again for the Warriors. They traded him to the New York Knicks over a year later, in 1999.

Few teams have had as bad of a five-year period as the Warriors did from 1997 to 2002. They never won more than 21 games in any of those seasons and the playoffs were out of reach. That five-year stretch was part of a dismal 12 years of not making the playoffs. That was the fourth-longest such streak in NBA history.

Golden State's management had problems. The biggest issue was that they kept getting talented young players but were unable to keep them. This happened with Antawn Jamison and Gilbert Arenas, who went on to become All-Stars with other teams.

To help their future, Golden State looked to its past. The Warriors hired Chris Mullin as their general manager in 2004. Mullin got to work making deals, deciding to build the team around guard Jason Richardson. The Warriors had picked Richardson fifth in the 2001 NBA Draft. In 2005, Mullin drafted guard

Monta Ellis slips between the San Antonio Spurs' Tim Duncan, *left*, and Tony Parker in 2006.

Monta Ellis and traded to get star guard Baron Davis.

Mullin hired Don Nelson as coach for the 2006–07 season. That year, Mullin also traded to get forwards Stephen Jackson and Al Harrington. Although the team had a losing record deep into the season, the Warriors finished strong with 16 wins in their last 21 games. They made the playoffs with a 42–40 record, and were seeded eighth in the Western Conference.

To begin the playoffs, the Warriors faced the Dallas Mavericks. The Mavericks had the NBA's best record and were seeded first. The teams split the first two games in Dallas, and then the Warriors won Games 3 and 4 in California. Dallas took Game 5, but the

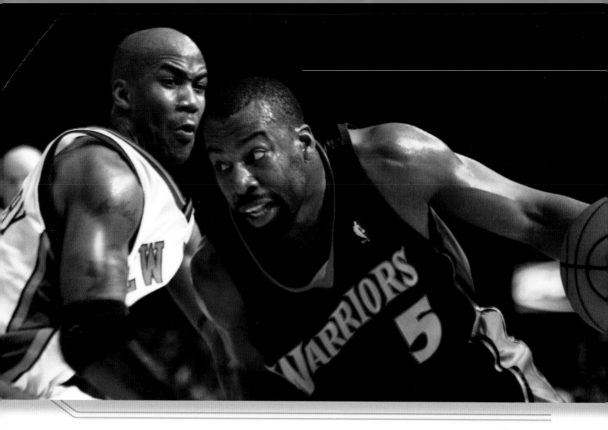

Baron Davis, *right*, dribbles past the New York Knicks' Stephon Marbury in 2005. Davis spent parts of four seasons with the Warriors.

Warriors won 111–86 in Game 6 and advanced to the Western Conference semifinals. Stephen Jackson poured in 33 points in Game 6. Davis added 20 more.

The Warriors were the first team seeded eighth to beat a team seeded first in a seven-game playoff series in NBA history. But their run ended there. They lost in five games to the Utah Jazz in the next round. In 2007–08, the Warriors improved their record by six games. But Golden State missed the playoffs. Eight teams in the West had 50 wins. The Warriors had 48 wins, but were shut out of the playoffs even though they had a better record than five of the Eastern Conference's playoff teams.

Davis then signed with the Los Angeles Clippers, Ellis

missed much of the 2008–09 season with injuries, and Richardson was traded to the Charlotte Bobcats. Without their prime players, Golden State failed to break 30 wins in each of the next two seasons. In 2009, Mullin was asked not to come back. And Nelson resigned as coach during preseason training camp in 2010.

The 2010–11 season was one of change for the Warriors. Keith Smart was named head coach. The team added new players including rookie Ekpe Udoh, free agent Dorell Wright, and rebounding machine David Lee.

Behind those players and young standouts Ellis, Wright, and second-year point guard Stephen Curry, the team appeared ready for a trip to the postseason. However, even with new players and a new coach, the Warriors only managed to finish

## Monta Ellis

Monta Ellis is fast. He is speedy on the court, but he also started his career quickly. He came to the NBA right out of high school and was drafted by Golden State in the second round in 2005. After Jason Richardson was traded, the Warriors signed Ellis to a long-term contract. He is a key piece of their future. Ellis was only 25 during 2010–11, his sixth NBA season. Although he was bothered by injuries he suffered during a moped accident in 2008, he has improved his play and his statistics steadily. In the 2009–10 season, he was one of only four players in the league to average 25 points and five assists per game.

36–46, missing the playoffs for the fourth time in four years.

After the season, the team parted ways with Smart. With new leadership and a young team led by Ellis, Wright, and Curry—the team's top three in scoring, assists, and steals in 2010–11—the Golden State Warriors hope to return to success in the future.

# TIMELINE

| 1946 | The Philadelphia Warriors make their BAA debut on November 7, defeating the Pittsburgh Ironmen 81–75. |
| --- | --- |
| 1947 | The Warriors win the first BAA championship on April 22, with an 83–80 win over the Chicago Stags in the fifth game of the BAA Finals. Forward Joe Fulks stars. |
| 1956 | The Philadelphia Warriors defeat the Fort Wayne Pistons 99–88 to capture their second championship. The title is their first as a member of the NBA. |
| 1959 | The Warriors take Wilt Chamberlain as a territorial draft pick. Chamberlain would set multiple scoring records in his Hall of Fame NBA career with the Warriors, the Philadelphia 76ers, and the Los Angeles Lakers. |
| 1962 | The Warriors relocate across the country, from Philadelphia, Pennsylvania to San Francisco, California. They become the San Francisco Warriors and move from the NBA's Eastern Division to the Western Division. |
| 1964 | San Francisco loses in the NBA Finals to the Boston Celtics. The Celtics win the series in five games to capture their sixth championship in a row, and seventh in eight years. |
| 1965 | San Francisco selects Rick Barry with the second pick in the NBA Draft on May 6. Barry spent most of his Hall of Fame career with the Warriors. |
| 1967 | The Warriors drop the NBA Finals to the Philadelphia 76ers in six games. Former Warriors coach Alex Hannum, the coach, and Wilt Chamberlain help lead Philadelphia to victory. |

**1970**
Al Attles coaches his first game for the Warriors on January 29. A former player, Attles would have a long career as the Warriors' coach and general manager.

**1971**
The team plays its first home game as the Golden State Warriors, in Oakland, against the Detroit Pistons on October 23. The Warriors win in overtime, 115–109.

**1975**
Golden State sweeps the Washington Bullets in the NBA Finals. The deciding Game 4 is a 96–95 win on May 25. It is the third and most recent league championship in franchise history.

**1985**
The team drafts Chris Mullin with the seventh pick in the NBA Draft on June 18. Mullin would go on to make five All-Star teams and play on the world-famous Dream Team in the 1992 Summer Olympics.

**1997**
During a December 1 practice, Golden State's Latrell Sprewell attacks coach P. J. Carlesimo during a practice. Sprewell is suspended for the rest of the season by the NBA and never plays another game for the Warriors.

**2010**
Don Nelson overtakes Lenny Wilkens as the NBA's winningest coach with a victory on April 7, 2010. The victory is the 1,333rd win of his career. Nelson's tenure as coach of the Warriors would come to an end when he resigns prior to the 2010–11 season. Nelson has a career record of 1,335-1,063 in 31 seasons as coach.

**2011**
The Warriors go 36–46 and miss the playoffs for the fourth time in four years. Coach Keith Smart is fired after his first season with the team.

# QUICK STATS

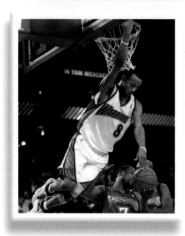

## FRANCHISE HISTORY
Philadelphia Warriors (1946–62)
San Francisco Warriors (1962–71)
Golden State Warriors (1971– )

## NBA FINALS
*(1950– ; wins in bold)*
1956, 1964, 1967, **1975**

## BAA FINALS
*(1946–49; win in bold)*
**1947**, 1948

## KEY PLAYERS
*(position[s]; years with team)*
Paul Arizin (G/F; 1950–52, 1954–62)
Rick Barry (F; 1965–67, 1972–78)
Wilt Chamberlain (C; 1959–65)
Monta Ellis (G; 2005– )

Joe Fulks (F/C; 1946–54)
Chris Mullin (G/F; 1985–97, 2000–01)
Robert Parish (C; 1976–80)
Nate Thurmond (F/C; 1963–74)

## KEY COACHES
Al Attles (1970–83):
    557–518; 31–30 (postseason)
Edward Gottlieb (1946–55):
    263–318; 15–17 (postseason)
Don Nelson (1988–95; 2006–10):
    422–443; 14–21 (postseason)

## HOME ARENAS
Philadelphia Arena (1946–62)
Philadelphia Convention Hall
    (1952–62)
San Francisco Civic Auditorium
    (1964–66)
University of San Francisco War
    Memorial Gymnasium (1964–66)
Cow Palace (1962–64, 1966–71 and
    two games in 1975 NBA Finals)
San Jose Arena (1996–97)
Oakland-Alameda County Coliseum
    Arena (1966–96, 1997– )
    Also known as Oracle Arena, The
    Arena in Oakland, and Oakland
    Arena

* All statistics through 2010–11 season

When Rick Barry walked to the free-throw line, he set up with the ball near his knees. Almost everyone shoots free throws overhand, but Barry started with the ball down low and pitched it underhanded toward the basket. It worked for him, though. He shot 89 percent from the line during his career and led the NBA in free-throw percentage six times. When Barry retired, he had the best career free-throw percentage, but he has since been passed by Mark Price and Steve Nash.

After his playing career, Wilt Chamberlain was involved in many different things. He was a successful businessman who owned a nightclub. He wrote several books, and he appeared in the movie *Conan the Destroyer* opposite Arnold Schwarzenegger. He also took up volleyball and became president of the International Volleyball Association.

For the NBA's 50th anniversary in 1996, the league released a list of its 50 Greatest Players. Six Warriors made the list: Paul Arizin, Barry, Chamberlain, Jerry Lucas, Robert Parish, and Nate Thurmond. Don Nelson was also picked as one of the top 10 coaches of all time. One of the voters who helped determine the list was longtime Warriors coach Al Attles.

The Warriors have had a blue and gold color scheme throughout their history, with various logos and uniform styles over the years. Recently they had a blue-tinted warrior holding a lightning bolt like a spear. In 2010, the logo became a circle with the Golden Gate Bridge in yellow on a blue background.

# GLOSSARY

**assist**

A pass that leads directly to a made basket.

**broadcaster**

An announcer who describes or talks about sporting events on television or radio.

**contract**

A binding agreement about, for example, years of commitment by a basketball player in exchange for a given salary.

**draft**

A system used by professional sports leagues to select new players in order to spread incoming talent among all teams. The NBA Draft is held each June.

**dynamic**

Energetic; forceful.

**general manager**

The executive who is in charge of the team's overall operation. He or she hires and fires coaches, drafts players, and signs free agents.

**overtime**

A period in a basketball game that is played to determine a winner when the four quarters end in a tie.

**postseason**

The games in which the best teams play after the regular-season schedule has been completed.

**rebound**

To secure the basketball after a missed shot.

**retire**

To officially end one's career.

**rookie**

A first-year player in the NBA.

**trade**

A move in which a player or players are sent from one team to another.

**veteran**

An individual with great experience in a particular endeavor.

# FOR MORE INFORMATION

## Further Reading

Barry, Rick. *Rick Barry's Super Sports Trivia Game*. Garden City Park, NY: Square One Publisher, 2004.

Cherry, Robert Allen. *Wilt: Larger Than Life*. Chicago, IL: Triumph Books, 2004.

Simmons, Bill. *The Book of Basketball: The NBA According to the Sports Guy*. New York: Random House, 2009.

## Web Links

To learn more about the Golden State Warriors, visit ABDO Publishing Company online at **www.abdopublishing.com.** Web sites about the Warriors are featured on our Book Links page. These links are routinely monitored and updated to provide the most current information available.

## Places To Visit

**Cow Palace**
2600 Geneva Avenue
Daly City, CA 94014
415-404-4100
www.cowpalace.com
This facility was the home of the Warriors from 1962 to 1964, and again from 1966 to 1971. These days, it plays host to various entertainment and sporting events.

**Naismith Memorial Basketball Hall of Fame**
1000 West Columbus Avenue
Springfield, MA 01105
413-781-6500
www.hoophall.com
This hall of fame and museum highlights the greatest players and moments in the history of basketball. Joe Fulks and Rick Barry are among the former Warriors enshrined here.

**Oracle Arena**
7000 Coliseum Way
Oakland, CA 94621
510-569-2121
www.coliseum.com
This has been the Warriors' home arena since 1966. It was renovated in 1997. The team plays 41 regular-season games here each year.

# INDEX

## About The Author

Rob Tricchinelli is a former newspaper copy editor and aspiring lawyer. He used to work for the sports section of the *Baltimore Sun* and the metro section of the *Washington Post*. Tricchinelli has also worked for National Public Radio's legal department and has written freelance news and sports stories in Maryland. He is currently based in the Washington DC area.